Everyone's Tao Te Ching

The Tao Te Ching for Those of Us Who Just Want to Find the Way

INTERPRETED BY

R. JOSEPH OWLES

2020 © *EVERYONE'S TAO TE CHING* – R. Joseph Owles

No part of this book may be reproduced, stored in a retrieval system, or transmitted by any means without the written permission of the author.

*Dedicated to
Kaiser and Lucas*

Contents

A WORD ABOUT THE TRANSLATION 1
INTRODUCTION 7
   A VERY BRIEF HISTORY OF THE TAO TE CHING 7
   KEY IDEAS EXPRESSED IN THE TAO TE CHING 13
      Tao 13
      Te 13
      Yin and Yang 14
      Going With the Flow (Wei Wu Wei) 15
      The Uncarved Block of Wood (Pu) 16
      The Three Treasures 16
BOOK OF PROCESS 19
   CHAPTER 1 20
   CHAPTER 2 23
   CHAPTER 3 25
   CHAPTER 4 27
   CHAPTER 5 29
   CHAPTER 6 31
   CHAPTER 7 32
   CHAPTER 8 33
   CHAPTER 9 34
   CHAPTER 10 36
   CHAPTER 11 38

CHAPTER 12 39

CHAPTER 13 41

CHAPTER 14 44

CHAPTER 15 46

CHAPTER 16 48

CHAPTER 17 50

CHAPTER 18 52

CHAPTER 19 53

CHAPTER 20 54

CHAPTER 21 57

CHAPTER 22 59

CHAPTER 23 60

CHAPTER 24 61

CHAPTER 25 63

CHAPTER 26 65

CHAPTER 27 66

CHAPTER 28 67

CHAPTER 29 69

CHAPTER 30 70

CHAPTER 31 72

CHAPTER 32 74

CHAPTER 33 75

CHAPTER 34 76

CHAPTER 35 77

CHAPTER 36 78

CHAPTER 37 79

THE BOOK OF POWER 80

CHAPTER 38 81

CHAPTER 39 84

CHAPTER 40 86

CHAPTER 41 87

CHAPTER 42 89

CHAPTER 43 90

CHAPTER 44 91

CHAPTER 45 92

CHAPTER 46 93

CHAPTER 47 94

CHAPTER 48 95

CHAPTER 49 96

CHAPTER 50 97

CHAPTER 51 99

CHAPTER 52 100

CHAPTER 53 102

CHAPTER 54 104

CHAPTER 55 106

CHAPTER 56 108

CHAPTER 57 110

CHAPTER 58 112

CHAPTER 59 113

CHAPTER 60 114

CHAPTER 61 115

CHAPTER 62 117

CHAPTER 63 119

CHAPTER 64 120

CHAPTER 65 122

CHAPTER 66 123

CHAPTER 67 124

CHAPTER 68 126

CHAPTER 69 127

CHAPTER 70 128

CHAPTER 71 129

CHAPTER 72 130

CHAPTER 73 131

CHAPTER 74 132

CHAPTER 75 134

CHAPTER 76 135

CHAPTER 77 136

CHAPTER 78 138

CHAPTER 79 140

CHAPTER 80 142

CHAPTER 81 144

INDEX **145**

A WORD ABOUT THE TRANSLATION

"All translation is interpretation." One of my professors in graduate school beat those words into my head over and over. We like to think of translations as an objective activity, but it is one that is highly interpretive. Every translator must make decisions. A translator must choose which words to use and how to structure those words into sentences and paragraphs. Each of those decisions can greatly affect the end result of the translation. And that would be true if we were translating in a vacuum, as if translating was purely an objective and antiseptic activity, void of personal perspectives and biases. It is not!

The truth is we put something of ourselves into the translation. Each of us have presuppositions and biases that bleed into the final product. We also may have an agenda that finds its way into the document. Some attempt to limit individual bias by employing the use of a group to translate. The group, it is thought, can keep any one individual from asserting her own views too strongly. Nevertheless, even groups are not without presuppositions and biases, and they make it into the translations. So, whether the translation is done by an individual or by a group, it is just as interpretive, just as biased, just as filled with agendas and presuppositions. All translations are imperfect. There are no perfectly objective, impartial translations of anything. There are only interpretations.

How is this process of interpretive translating done? Well, generally speaking, there are two methods of translation. They are termed "literal translation" and "dynamic equivalent." Literal translations are what the name implies: an attempt to convey the words from one language into corresponding or equivalent words into a different language. Most literal translations not only attempt to convey a word-for-word translation of the original text, they also attempt to maintain word order from the original as well. Therefore, the goal is to render the document in vocabulary, style, structure, etc. from one language into another. Dynamic equivalent, on the other hand, is a method of translation that focuses more on conveying meaning rather than conveying the actual words or literary structure. In this method, the translator is not focused on rendering a word for word translation, but rather is attempting to discern the meaning of the text written in one language and rendering that meaning into the language and idioms of a different language.

So, literal translations may sacrifice meaning in the pursuit of accurately capturing the words and structure, while dynamic equivalent may sacrifice the words and the structure to capture the meaning. Which one is better? It depends on what you want. Do you want to know what the text says, or do you want to know what the text means? If the former, then you want a literal translation; if the latter, then you want a dynamic equivalent.

The fact of the matter is that the most literal of literal translations must infuse some dynamic equivalent into them or else the text would make no sense. Different languages are... well... different. They employ different sentence structure, use adjectives differently, and use words in a different way. Translation is not as simple as plugging in the words from one language into another because it would, in most circumstances, result in a jumble of words. Then you would have to translate the translation to determine how to understand what all those words mean. That is just negotiating the sentence structure. Words are not always easy to translate. Words do not always have a one-to-one correspondence among differing languages. The simple truth is that words do not have meaning, they have context. The meaning of a word is affected by how it is used. Someone can use the word "dog" and mean a furry, four-legged animal. That understanding of the word "dog" may be accurate ninety percent of the time. Yet, if the same person is playing poker and calls another person a "dirty dog," that person is not being called an unwashed, furry, four-legged animal, but is, in fact, being called a cheat and a scoundrel. Same word, different meaning.

So, all of that was to say that most translations are a compromise of a literal translation and a dynamic equivalent. They may lean toward one more than the other, but chances are they contain elements of both. The compromise is that most translations, even contemporary language translations, still seek to maintain the sentence structure and vocabulary as much as possible, but they resort to capturing the meaning in those places were a literal translation cannot work.

Translating *THE TAO TE CHING* presents the usual challenges of translation while posing its own: its brevity. The entire text is comprised of only five thousand Chinese characters. An example of the difficulties of a literal translation appear in the very first line of the text which literally reads: "Tao can Tao not eternal Tao." Perhaps it works better in Chinese, but in English, it seems to lack something. So, we have to fill in some of the meaning.

The brevity of the text may make it difficult to translate, but it is also what gives it its charm and its power. There are as many translations and understandings of *THE TAO TE CHING* as there are people reading it. The brevity of the text creates an intentional vagueness, which in turn creates the need to meditate on the text to discern meaning from it. But the meaning is not static. You may meditate on the text today and find some practical insight and twenty years later discover some new insight from the same text. Also, you may meditate on the text and find no value or insight in it, only to discover value or insight at some later time. The text is 2,500 years old and appears static because it exists as a finalized document. Yet, as old and as finalized as the document may be, it continues to change and be new because we are always a different person when we read it. The fact that it does not simply tell you what it means but requires you to figure it out is why so many of us keep going back to the text, but it is also what makes translating the text difficult.

EVERYONE'S TAO TE CHING is a snapshot in time. I translated the text over a decade ago and published it under the title PROCESS OF POWER, thinking then that "Process" was the best way to translate Tao. I thought it was a good translation then, and I still think it is mostly a good translation, but I have changed, and my understanding of the text has changed. So, I present *EVERYONE'S TAO TE CHING* as a possible understanding of the text. It is not perfect, but what is? It is not the definitive translation. It is merely mine.

My goal in translating the text in the manner in which I do in *EVERYONE'S TAO TE CHING,* was not only to capture the possible meaning of the words, but also to capture some of the humor and personality of Lao Tzu as it comes across. There is a tendency to view our religious and philosophical teachers as unsmiling, serious, unemotional automatons. Very few Christians, for instance, seem to view Jesus as a person who laughed or even smiled. He was just sober and serious as he handed down the Word of God. I view both Jesus and Lao Tzu as laughers. I often hear in both their words a gentle teasing, a nudging through humor and good-natured joking. My style of translation sought to capture that sort of approach to teaching. It is translated as a teacher talking to a student. The teacher is sometimes serious and mysterious, but at other times, he is humorous and teasing.

EVERYONE'S TAO TE CHING is a blend of dynamic equivalent, commentary, and personal insight. It is meant to be as simple as possible and as understandable as possible, while understanding that the endeavor for simplicity and understandability may affect the accuracy. There are many translations of *THE TAO TE CHING* available. I suggest you examine them and compare them. This is one possible translation in a sea of translations. It is a single drop of water in a flood. My hope is that it is the drop of water that satisfies your thirst. My hope is that it may not help you find the answers as much as it helps you to understand the questions. My hope is that you find value in this translation, knowing that I may be wrong in my translation and you may be wrong in your understanding of it, or that we both could be right, but just seeing that rightness from different places.

INTRODUCTION

A VERY BRIEF HISTORY OF THE TAO TE CHING

The *TAO TE CHING*, or the *LAO TZU,* as the text was originally known, provides the basis for Taoism. The writing of the *TAO TE CHING* is traditionally associated with the semi-historical figure of Lao Tzu.[1] Little, if anything, truly historical is known about Lao Tzu's existence. There have been many attempts to link Lao Tzu with actual historical figures, the most common being that of the Chou historian Li Er.[2] According to tradition, Li Er is said to have served as the chief historian and archivist for the region of Chou during a turbulent period of Chinese history referred to as

---

[1] Lao Tzu is not a proper name but a title meaning "Old Master." Lao Tzu may also be read as a plural (Old Masters), which would make it the work the product of many writers and teachers and not the product of one, particular person. The word Tzu also occasionally carries the connotation of "child," making the author the "Old Child," a possible allusion to, or the source of, the mythical account of Lao Tzu emerging from his mother's womb as an old man.

[2] It appears that this "historical" figure may be the product of legend as well. The name Li Er means "Long Ear-lobed Li," referring to an ancient Chinese belief that the size of one's earlobes was demonstrative of the quantity of one's possession of wisdom. The longer the earlobes, the wiser the person was thought to be. Therefore, Li Er can be rendered "Very Wise Li."

the Spring and Autumn Period of the Eastern Chou dynasty (c. 722 B.C.E. – c. 481 B.C.E.). Tradition also asserts that after a long career, and after developing a reputation for wisdom, Li Er became increasingly dissatisfied living in a civilization that was in decline, so he set off for the Western wilderness. Before he could leave civilization, forever disappearing into the wilderness, a border patrolman asked him to write down the bulk of his teachings. This he did, writing out a volume of his teaching in two books, which was originally known simply as the *LAO TZU* after its purported author, but which is now better known as the *TAO TE CHING*.

The text of the *TAO TE CHING* is traditionally divided into two "books." Book One contains the first thirty-seven chapters, while Book Two comprises the remaining material. There is, however, no sense of structural, thematic, or literary cohesion that justifies such a division.[3] The division of the text into two books seems to have mainly come about as a means of confirming the tradition that Lao Tzu wrote two books. Nevertheless, the division of Lao Tzu's writing into the two books, the *TAO CHING* and the *TE CHING* goes back at least to the first century C.E. and eventually gives rise to the title of *TAO TE CHING* sometime

---

3. For that matter, there often does not appear to be any thematic cohesion within the various chapters themselves.

in the second century C.E. when referring to the work as a whole.

Assigning a date to the writing of the TAO TE CHING is difficult due to the general lack of information regarding its authorship. If the tradition of Lao Tzu being an older contemporary of Confucius is correct, then he would have been born before Confucius. The figure of Confucius allows for some level of historical certainty regarding dates. It is generally accepted that Confucius lived sometime around 552 – 479 B.C.E., which would push Lao Tzu's birth back to around 600 B.C.E., establishing the writing of the TAO TE CHING to have occurred somewhere in the early to middle sixth century B.C.E. This tradition, however, does not correspond with the consensus of contemporary literary criticism, which places the time of authorship closer to the fourth century B.C.E. rather than the sixth. If Lao Tzu was the author of the TAO TE CHING and also an older contemporary of Confucius, how could he then write the book in the fourth century B.C.E.? The answer suggests one of two possibilities. Either Lao Tzu lived much later than tradition asserts, or Lao Tzu was not the author of the TAO TE CHING.[4] Given the lack of verifiable information, the best

---

4. Logic does allow for other possibilities. It could be that Lao Tzu wrote a sixth century B.C.E. version of the *Tao Te Ching* to which material was added and older material was rewritten. It could also be that Lao Tzu lived an extraordinarily long life, ranging close to two centuries. It could also be that the author of the *Tao Te Ching* was projected back to the sixth century and

evidence of literary criticism, as well as the thematic and literary diversity within the text, the best way to explain the time of authorship may be merely to accept that the *TAO TE CHING* is a collection of aphoristic sayings that were predominately compiled in the fourth century B.C.E., but which ultimately ranges from the sixth to the third centuries B.C.E.[5] If this is true, then this would place the bulk of its authorship within the period of Chinese history known as the Warring States Period.

The Warring States Period was a time of intense rivalry and almost constant warfare among the many states that comprised a disunited China. The turbulence of the time produced many philosophical attempts to explain and fix the often chaotic events and circumstances. The two most long-lived traditions to emerge from this period were Confucianism and Taoism.

---

made a contemporary of Confucius to give him a greater sense of philosophical authority. Priority should probably be given to this final logical solution when one takes into account the mutual rivalry and criticism that existed between Taoists and Confucians.

5. This, of course, makes the text the product of many authors and editors over the period of many centuries. Therefore, for the sake of simplicity any references to authorship will simply be the traditional Lao Tzu, even though it is to be accepted that there were likely many hands in the final product.

Confucianism understood the universe as possessing a moralistic foundation, which could be experienced and expressed through the practice of certain prescribed behaviors. For Confucians, there was an underlying "should-ness" that supported the fabric of the universe. This should-ness required a corresponding ethical[6] expression. A system of ritual and personal conduct could be developed that reflected a particular moralistic imperative, such as "you *should* respect authority." Confucianism was social in its focus and in its application.

Taoism denied any idea of a fundamental moralistic reality undergirding the universe. For the Taoist, there was no *should*. There was only *is*. For instance, geese do not migrate south for the winter because they *should*, but because that is the way it *is*. That is what geese do. The absence of a moralistic quality supporting the universe did not negate ethical expression. On the contrary, the Taoist believed that the best way to behave was in agreement with the fundamental "is-ness" of the universe. The Taoists believed that rules for proper etiquette and moralistic standards resulted because people have cut themselves off from nature and have forgotten the way the universe is. If people would instead act according to the "is-ness" of

---

6. Although the term ethics is often employed as a synonym for morality, the term here is meant to be more precise. Ethics here is to be understood as a system of behavior.

nature, then they would naturally behave in a manner that is socially good.

EVERYONE'S TAO TE CHING

KEY IDEAS EXPRESSED IN THE TAO TE CHING

Tao

The Chinese character *Tao* is usually translated "way." *Tao* has many of the nuances that the word "way" does in English. It can be synonymous with a characteristic: "That is the way something is." It can be synonymous with a path or direction: "What is the best way to get to your house?" It can be synonymous with a particular course of circumstances: "That is the way it goes." Specifically, in Taoists texts, *Tao* refers to the way the universe works or unfolds. *Tao* is universal process.

In the West, many thinkers attempt to link the idea of *Tao* with God. *Tao* is not God. It is the process by which the universe has come into being and It is the reality that sustains the universe, but It cannot be spoken of as "Creator" since that term implies not only action but also purpose and intent. The *Tao* has no purpose or intention for the universe. It is simply the means through which the universe has come into being and the means through which the universe continues.

Te

The character *Te* is often rendered "virtue"; yet, this is a faulty translation of the word due to the fact that "virtue" in English has taken on a decidedly moralistic connotation, usually having to do with a sense of moral correctness. This has little to do with the original meaning of *Te*, which was "power." This power is not necessarily the ability to coerce events and people, which is how power is often perceived in the West. Rather, the power of *Te* is the potential energy of being in the right place at the right time and in the right frame of mind. The power expressed in the *Tao Te Ching* is a potentiality that occurs apart from human intervention. *Te* is the manifestation of *Tao*. The power of *Tao* is in Its action. To cultivate *Te*, or power, is to live in accordance with *Tao*.

Yin and Yang

In Chinese thought, there is a unity in polarity. The *yin* and the *yang* refer to the shaded and the sunny sides of a hill. There is one hill, but there are two sides, each possessing distinct and differing qualities; yet, the hill cannot exist if either of its sides is missing because without the opposite side, the hill would collapse upon itself and cease to be. In the West, polarity is conceived as two opposing forces acting against each other: good versus bad; light versus dark; hot versus cold; loud versus quiet, and so on. In Taoist thought, however, the poles do not oppose but influence each other. For the Taoist it is not good versus bad, but both good and bad; it is light and dark; hot and cold; loud and quiet.

The intermingling of polar opposites is the creative force behind the universe. A child is created when the two poles of male and female come together. If male and female behave in the classic Western understanding of polarity, then they attempt to annihilate each other and there is no creative force that can produce offspring. The earth is full of life because the earth is full of polarity generating the creative force of life.

<u>Going With the Flow</u> *(Wei Wu Wei)*

The phrase *wei wu wei* literally means "Act empty act" or "act without acting." This "empty action" has often been misunderstood as justifying inaction or noninvolvement. This, however, is not the meaning of "empty action." Although not a literal translation, the most effective way of rendering *wei wu wei* into English is "go with the flow." The flow, of course, being the flow of *Tao*.

Going with the flow, then, is not inaction, but rather, a particular kind of action. It is a manner of acting in accordance with *Tao*. It is efficient action that does not waste time or effort in the attempt to force outcomes, or to constrain situations to be any way other than what they are. Quite simply, it is easier to swim with the current of a river than it is to swim against the current; it is easier to go with the flow rather than fight against the flow. *Tao* goes as *Tao* goes, and the Taoist goes along with it.

The Uncarved Block of Wood (Pu)

The uncarved block of wood is the Taoist symbol for unlimited potential. The word *Pu* refers to a thing in its natural condition. A block of wood, before it is carved, can be made into anything. A block of wood, however, that has been carved into an object can only be what that object is. The world is a world carved by perception, bias, bigotry, and expectation. The world is carved by the use of labels and stereotypes. The world is often understood to be such-and-such a way because labels and expectations force it to be that way. The model of the uncarved piece of wood is a challenge to strip away the labels, bigotries, biases, and expectations that are imposed upon the world, allowing the world to be what it is. The author of the *TAO TE CHING* took for granted what Voltaire would express nearly two thousand years later in a different part of the globe: "The greatest hindrance to our making an exact analysis of things is not that our minds are void of knowledge, as much as they are filled with bigotries."

The Three Treasures

The Three Treasures or the Three Jewels are "compassion," "frugality" or "moderation," and "humility." They form the bases of Taoist ethics.

Compassion. Compassion is love in action. The Chinese character can literally mean: "compassion," "tenderness," "love," "mercy," "kindness," "gentleness," and/or "benevolence." It has the sense of "mothering," "nurturing," and providing tender care. It is not an internal feeling of empathy. It is an action.

Moderation. It can literally mean: "frugality," "moderation," or "restraint." Again, this is not an inward feeling but an outward action. Moderation is the activity of not wasting anything. It is living simply. It is a life that restrains being motivated by desire, but instead, being motivated by simple, efficient action that values everything and wastes nothing. It is an avoidance of excess and extremes. It promotes generosity by not hoarding or collecting more than is needed.

Humility. The use of "humility" is a translation of six Chinese Characters (不敢為天下先) which means something like: "dare not to be first." It may correspond to the mantra of Captain Spock in *THE WRATH OF KHAN* which states: "The needs of the many outweigh the needs of the few, or the one." Not putting oneself first is to refrain from putting self-interest first. It is to refrain from acting and speaking from ego and personal agenda. It is sacrificing the need to be right and to win.

These Three Jewels: to live gently, expressing kindness, mercy, love for all things; to live simply, valuing everything and wasting nothing, avoiding excess and extremes; and putting the needs of others above the needs of oneself is the basis of Taoist behavior and ethics. Like water, they appear simply and weak. And yet, like water, they have the strength to wear away stone and dig deep canyons.

EVERYONE'S TAO TE CHING

BOOK OF PROCESS

CHAPTER 1

When you know,
You don't know.
When you know that you don't know,
You begin to know.

You can understand,
But you don't understand.
When you understand that you don't understand,
You begin to understand.

If you know it,
It's not Tao.
Tao is infinite and eternal.
It's bigger than what you can know or understand.

You can describe it,
But It can't be described.
When you say that you can't describe it,
You begin to describe it.

If you can describe it,
It's not Tao.
Tao is infinite and eternal.
It's bigger than your vocabulary.

EVERYONE'S TAO TE CHING

Tao is infinite and eternal.
It made heaven and earth.
Don't try to figure out how.
It's beyond your comprehension.
Even if you could understand It,
You wouldn't be able to articulate It.

Everything that lives and everything that exists
Does so because of Tao.
They change, adapt, reproduce.
We can figure out the hows and the whys of some of it.
We can identify the patterns
And manipulate the processes.
But we don't know it all.
It's bigger than us and what we can know.

Get out of your head and get out of your own way!
Give up your desires
And you'll see how everything is connected.
Hold on to your desires
And you will realize why everything behaves as it does –
Because everything is motivated by desire.

Was that an inconsistency?
Maybe.
Are "giving up" and "holding on" contradictory?
Perhaps.
Are they somehow the same thing?

EVERYONE'S TAO TE CHING

Yes!
Is it beyond understanding?
Definitely!

Embrace it!
In that apparent contradiction lies truth.
Tao is paradox and contradiction.
Tao is the doorway that leads to wisdom

CHAPTER 2

When you decide that one thing is beautiful
You make something else ugly.

When you decide that one thing is good
You make something else bad.

By establishing the one
You inadvertently establish the other.

So, by making one thing,
You make its opposite at the same time.

Think about it.
There can be no "something" without "nothing."
There can be no "easy" without "difficult."
There can be no "long" without "short."
There can be no "high" without "low."
There can be no sound without silence.
Something can only lead when something else follows.

So, wise up!
Go with the flow!
Teach others by doing and not by talking.

Everything that exists flows from Tao.
Tao is the source of all of it.

EVERYONE'S TAO TE CHING

Yet, Tao does not bully or command.
Tao simply does what is necessary
And asks nothing in return.
Tao does what needs to be done
And takes no credit for it.

CHAPTER 3

Show favoritism,
And you will create jealousy and resentment.
Hoard what you consider to be of great value
And you will be robbed.
Decide that it is your way or the highway,
And you will create discord and debate.

Wise up!
Learn to treat everything the same.
Don't favor one person over another.
Don't consider one thing more valuable than another.
Treat everyone and everything the same,
Without partiality or prejudice.

Wise up!
If you want to be a smart leader,
Don't try to convince others about good and bad.
Don't decide who is worthy and who is not.
Don't fill peoples' heads but fill their bellies.
Avoid ambition.
Show the strength of humility.
Don't give the people things to worry about.
Don't tell them things they don't need to know.
If that's how you lead,
Then greed and covetousness will be held in check,
And ambition and selfish rivalry will be diluted.

Wise up!
If you want to be a good leader,
Then govern, don't rule!
Don't insist on your own rules.
Don't make rules for the sake of having rules,
Don't seek to appease your own sense of power.
Lead by example not by decree!

Wise up!
Go with the flow!
Trust the people to be themselves.
Embrace the chaos of not knowing how it all works out.
There are many different individuals,
All behaving individually.
There are many different individuals,
All seeking their own individual needs and desires.
Don't micromanage them!
Trust them to be who they are.
Place who they are in the situation where they need to be.
And then let it all play out the way it is supposed to.

CHAPTER 4

Keep relying on Tao.
You'll never be disappointed.
You'll never run out!
The more you demand from It,
The more It supplies.

You look at Tao,
But you see nothing.
Tao looks empty even when full.
It is like water at the bottom of a bottomless well
That somehow rises up to replenish the world.
You look at It,
But you see nothing.
And yet, It is the source of all that is.
It appears empty,
Yet, It fills everything.

You can't embrace Tao,
Without embracing impermanence.
Nothing lasts forever.
No condition remains the same.
Even the sharpest blade is dulled by Tao.
The most tightly tangled knot is loosened by Tao.
The harshest glare is softened by Tao.
The well-traveled path is made where there is no path.

EVERYONE'S TAO TE CHING

That is Tao.
You look at It,
But nothing is there.
It offers hints that It is there
But It doesn't let you see It.
It likes to work behind the scenes.

I don't know where it came from.
It has just always been there.

CHAPTER 5

Wise up!
Don't show favoritism for anyone!
Everyone is mortal!
Mortality ultimately makes sacrifices of us all.

So, wise up!
Treat all people with the utmost respect,
Until they are sacrificed by time to death.
Honor the sacrifice,
And don't despair.

Heaven and earth
Never show favoritism for anything.
They know that everything is finite.
Finitude makes sacrifices of everything that exists.

Heaven and earth treat everything
With the highest respect,
Until they are sacrificed by time to nonexistence.
They honor the sacrifice
And they don't despair.

The space between heaven and earth is empty.
It is like the emptiness of a bellows used to stoke a fire.
It is empty; yet, it never runs out of air.
The more it is used, the more it produces.

Spout off your opinion
And you'll create arguments and enemies.
Talk too much
And you'll create awkward silences.
Wise up!
Avoid extremes!

CHAPTER 6

Life happens in the open, empty spaces.
Life is conceived and nurtured
In the empty space of the womb.
The open, emptiness is sometimes called
"The Indescribable Mother."
Just as everything that lives is born from a mother,
The Eternal Mother of the vast open, emptiness
Gives birth to everything that exists in heaven and earth.

Tao appears empty but It is full.
It is like water at the bottom of a bottomless well
That rises up to replenish the world.
You look at It,
But you see nothing.
It offers hints that It is there
But It doesn't let you see It.
It likes to work behind the scenes.
Keep relying on Tao.
You'll never be disappointed.
You'll never run out!
The more you demand from It,
The more It supplies.

CHAPTER 7

Heaven and earth last forever.
How can they last forever?
Because they don't live for themselves.
That's how they can last forever.

So, wise up!
Be like them!
Put yourself last
And find that you are first.
Stop worrying about your wants
And discover that you have everything you need.
Focus on the needs of others
And find that your needs are met as well.
Stop being motivated by self-centered fear,
But be motivated by other-centered love.

Wise up!
Stop being concerned only about yourself!
By making the needs of others important to you,
Your needs become important to them.

CHAPTER 8

The highest good is like water:
Water keeps everything healthy.
Everything needs water to live.
Water doesn't compete.
Water doesn't try to flow upward,
But settles in the lowest places
Where other things would resent being.
That's why water is a good model for Tao.

The value of a house
Depends on its location.
The value of a mind
Depends on its insight.
The value of an ally
Depends on his goodwill toward you.
The value of speech
Depends on its sincerity.
The value of a government
Depends on its ability to maintain order.
The value of any enterprise
Depends on the skill that goes into it.
The value of an action
Depends on its good timing.

Tao is perfect because It does not compete.

CHAPTER 9

Too much of a good thing will work against you.
A container that is too full spills its contents everywhere.
An empty container spills nothing.
An empty container without a flaw
Is better than a full container that leaks.

Nothing is permanent.
No matter how sharp you make the blade,
It will eventually become dull again.
You can't change it.
It's just the way it is.
Accept it!

You can fill your vault with expensive and beautiful items.
But you can never be sure that the treasure is safe.
No matter how secure the lock is,
No matter how many guards you hire,
Some thief will find a way to beat your security.

If you acquire a lot of wealth and prestige,
Then you're going to get cocky and arrogant.
Arrogance invites bad luck and bad luck invites disaster.

Heaven never wears out its welcome.
That is it's nature.

EVERYONE'S TAO TE CHING

It does what it needs to do
And then it leaves the second the task is completed.

CHAPTER 10

It's all a balancing act.
Walk with impermanence balanced on your head,
While holding permanence in your arms.
Walk without letting one fall and the other drop.

Be calm and still.
Be as gentle as a baby's breath.
Let your mind be as clear and transparent
As a window without a single smudge.

Love people whoever and however they are.
Lead them without ruling them.
Lead them without meddling in their affairs.
Be like the mother bird
And let the baby birds fly away from the nest.
Give people the freedom to make mistakes.
Give them the freedom to fail.

Just because you know what needs to be done,
It doesn't mean that you're the one to do it.
Just because you know what needs to be said,
It doesn't mean that you are the one to say it.
Just because you see something clearly,
It doesn't mean you get to tell others where to look
And what they must see.

EVERYONE'S TAO TE CHING

Tao gives everything life.
Tao nurtures them.
Tao gives everything life,
But It claims no authority over anything.
Tao assists everything,
But It never demands gratitude from anything.
Tao protects everything,
But It never demands obedience from anything.
Tao is power beyond power.
Tao is power beyond words.

CHAPTER 11

Thirty spokes converge in one hub.
It is the empty space that makes the wheel useful.

Clay is molded into a cup.
It is the empty space that makes the cup useful.

Doors and windows are empty spaces
Carved into a room.
The empty space is what makes a room a room.
If the room were solid,
It would not be a room and it would have no use.
It is the empty space that allows it to be useful.

So, we value the substance
Because the emptiness makes it useful.

CHAPTER 12

If you want everything,
You end up with nothing.
If you saw every color at once,
You'd be blinded.
If you heard every note at once,
You'd be deafened.
If you tasted every flavor at once,
You'd lose your sense of taste.

Running in circles and chasing your tail
Will drive you nuts.
Walking around with priceless treasure and wealth
Will get you robbed and killed.

So, wise up!
Focus on what is on the inside,
Not on what is on the outside.
Value substance rather than appearances!
Feed your hungry spirit
And don't just feed the many appetites of your body.
Stop chasing everything you want
And stop focusing on your own needs.
Stop chasing after what has no real value
And focus instead on what is truly valuable.
Wise up!
Stop looking at what you want.

Look instead at what you have.

Abandon the chase and you'll catch everything you need.

Know what is truly valuable.

Do this, and you will never be indecisive.

EVERYONE'S TAO TE CHING

CHAPTER 13

Praise is just as dangerous as disgrace.
Don't seek one and avoid the other.
Avoid both equally.
Care about what causes you trouble
As if it were your own body.

"That's crazy!" you say.
"What do you mean by saying:
'Praise is just as dangerous as disgrace.
Don't seek one and avoid the other.
Avoid both equally'?

I simply mean that favor gained now
Is favor that eventually will be lost.
When you are favored,
You live in the fear of losing favor.
When favor is lost,
You experience the same distress as being disgraced,
Even though no disgrace has occurred.
That's why I say:
"Praise is just as dangerous as disgrace."
That is why I advise:
"Avoid both equally."

Then you ask me:
"But what could you possibly mean by saying:

EVERYONE'S TAO TE CHING

'Care about what causes you trouble
As if it were your own body'"?
I simply means that I have great trouble
Because I concern myself with the needs of my body.
If I had no body, I would have no trouble.
What troubles would I have if I had no body to care for?
So, the less I seek to satisfy the cravings of my body,
The fewer troubles I have in my life.
The more I get out of myself,
The more peace I have.

Who can you trust to govern the nation?
Someone who has self-control,
But who is not self-centered.
Someone who has no ambitions,
And who has no desire for political power.
Someone who can govern his own life,
And keep his own affairs in order,
Without being concerned about self-seeking gain,
And who cares nothing about power and prestige.
That is the person you can trust to govern a nation.

Who can you hand over the running of the country to?
Someone who loves self-control
More than he loves political power.
Someone who cares about governing himself
More than he cares about ruling others –

EVERYONE'S TAO TE CHING

That is the person who deserves to be in charge.
You can just hand the entire country over to him.

CHAPTER 14

You can look at Tao,
But you can't see It.
Even if you get a glimpse of It,
You'll never see It clearly.
That is why we can't describe It accurately.

You can listen for Tao,
But you can't hear It.
Even if you could hear a little of It,
You wouldn't hear It clearly.
That is why we say It is silent.

You can reach for Tao,
But you can't touch It.
You can grope for It,
But you'll never hold It or pin It down.
That's why we say It is intangible.

Get out of your head and turn off your brain!
You'll never understand these three things.
This is not something you can work out in your head.
It is more about experiencing than it is about knowing.

Because you can't understand each of these three,
They blend into a single mystery.

Tao is neither more radiant when rising,
Nor is It darker when descending.
Tao is like a deep, dark well.
If you peer into it, you can't see the bottom.
It is a nameless name.
It comes from nothing and returns to nothingness.
It is the shapeless shape.
It is the image of nothingness.
It has no tangible form, borders, or boundaries.
It is a shadow you see in the corner of your eye.
No one knows where Tao comes from.
You wouldn't know It even if you were looking at It.
If you were to walk up to It,
You wouldn't see Its front.
If you followed behind It,
You wouldn't see Its back.

Cling to the ancient Tao of old,
And you can master the affairs of the present.
Know the Ancient Source
And know the essence of the present Tao.

CHAPTER 15

There are those who lived long ago,
Who knew Tao in the most ancient of days.
How can I describe those people?
They were mysterious and vague.
They were filled with deep, abiding wisdom.
They were too bewildering to be understood,
Defying any attempt to label or pigeonhole them.

At best, I can only offer and inexact description.
They were nebulous and so bewildering
That they defy clear cut descriptions and categories.

Off the top of my head
I would say that they were cautious and focused,
As if they were crossing a deep, fast-moving river.
They were restrained,
As if they were avoiding the gossip of their neighbors.
They were always on their best behavior,
As if they were guests in somebody's home.
They appeared weak and yielding like melting ice.
They were as unrefined as an uncarved piece of wood.
They were as expansive as a valley.
They were as murky as muddy water.

EVERYONE'S TAO TE CHING

Water is murky when it is stirred up
But when it settles and is still,
It becomes clear.

A sleeping person is as still as the dead.
He knows nothing while he is sleeping.
Yet, he knows how to wake up when the time is right.
He does not make it happen.
It happens because he knows how to let it happen.

Empty yourself if you want to cling to Tao.
Be like an old garment –
Well-worn and full of holes.
And yet, be brand new at the same time.

CHAPTER 16

If you can empty yourself of yourself,
There'll be space enough to be filled with serenity.

Everything that lives comes and goes.
They are many and I am one.
But we all spring from the same source.
And we all arrive at the same end.
When empty and serene,
I observe the births and the deaths,
The comings and the goings,
The origins from nothing,
And the return to nothing.
When I observe all of this,
I comprehend the meaning of the word "serenity."

Serenity simply means being reconciled to your fate.
When you are reconciled to your fate,
You become persistent.
When you become persistent,
You become wise.

But resisting your fate,
Makes you stupid.
You behave recklessly.

If you keep behaving recklessly,
Your life will be filled with misfortune.

If you want to endure, then you have to accept.
To accept, you must become unbiased.
To become unbiased, you must be impartial.
When you become impartial,
You will become majestic and regal.
When you become majestic and regal,
You will become like heaven.
When you become like heaven,
You will become like Tao.
When you become like Tao,
There can be no misfortune.
You'll always be safe and sound.

CHAPTER 17

The best kind of leader is aloof and distant.
He is like a silhouette in the distance.
He doesn't get involved in every detail.
He doesn't meddle in what everyone is doing.
He doesn't make himself the center of attention.
He just does his job and serves as an example.
He lets the people do their jobs and forget all about him.

The second-best kind of leader is loved.

The third-best kind of leader is feared.

The worst kind of leader is despised and ridiculed.

If you trust the people you lead,
Your trust will not be misplaced.
You make the people untrustworthy
By not trusting them,
And they will never trust you in return.

If you want to be the best kind of leader,
Don't issue decrees.
Don't make up a lot of rules and regulations.
Be the decree!
Be the rules and regulations!
Live them and embody them!

EVERYONE'S TAO TE CHING

Don't talk when you can do.
Do what needs to be done
The way it is supposed to be done.
By doing that,
You show people how to be and what to do.
You give them an example to follow
And every goal is achieved.
Then the people say:
"Look at all we accomplished on our own!"

CHAPTER 18

Whenever the Great Tao is forgotten or ignored,
Those in charge control the people
With religiosity and pietism.

Whenever truth and facts are ignored and twisted,
Giving way to cunning and cleverness,
Those in charge become corrupt
And govern with hypocrisy and pretense.

Whenever the family is in disarray,
Those in charge control the people
By appealing to "family values,"
And proclaiming the "sanctity of marriage,"
While defining what a family is and is not.

When a nation falls into chaos,
Those in charge control the people
By appealing to patriotic fervor.

CHAPTER 19

Get out of your head!
Give up your bigotries!
Stop deciding how people and things are supposed to be!
Everyone will be a lot better off when you do.
Throw away all your preconceived notions!

Get rid of religiosity and pietism!
Everyone will naturally do the right thing.
They will remember how to be compassionate.

Get rid of cleverness and cunning!
Abandon your desire for personal gain!
Then thieves and robbers will vanish from the nation.

But all that is only the start.
If nothing else is done,
They are cosmetic remedies at best.

If you want to change everything from the inside out,
People must give up extravagance and embrace simplicity.
They must limit their desires and stop being self-centered.

CHAPTER 20

When you're stuck in your head,
You're stuck in your worries.
That's where your worries live!
So, get out of your head
And you'll get out of your worries.

Who cares if you say "yes"
but they say "no"?
What difference does it really make?
Isn't your life the same
Whether they agree with you or not?

Who cares if you think something is good,
But they think it's bad?
What difference does it really make?
Isn't your life the same
Whether they agree with you or not?

And how far apart are you, really?
You only see the difference
And you miss what you have in common.

You don't have to worry about something
Just because others are worried about it.
You don't have to be afraid of something
Just because others fear it.

EVERYONE'S TAO TE CHING

You have the right to be your own person
And not get caught up in everyone else's stuff.
People feed off distractions and busywork.
No matter how busy they are,
They will always take the time
To stick their noses in other people's business.
They worry about not having enough to worry about.

I don't let myself get caught up in all that nonsense.
I remain tranquil and at peace.
I show no interest in any of that.
I am like a newborn baby
Who hasn't learned how to smile yet.
I don't let myself get tied down,
Wandering aimlessly like someone living on the streets.

People have more than they could possibly need.
I alone seem to be in need.
They think I am my possessions.
Because I have nothing,
They think I am nothing
And have nothing to offer.

People are clever and see things clearly.
I alone am confused.
People have goals and ambitions.
I appear unfocused and unmotivated.
I come and go like the waves of the sea.

I am as aimless as the wind.
People are busy trying to keep up with everyone else.
Because I could not care less about that,
They think I am uncouth and stupid.

I guess I'm just different.
I'm not like anyone else.
They find nourishment in gossip and status.
I find nourishment in Tao, the Mother of the World.

CHAPTER 21

If you really want to influence people and events
Then live Tao completely.
Be Tao in all you do.

What is Tao like?
The natural state of Tao looks like nothing
And feels like nothing is there.

It looks like nothing.
Yet, in the deepest part of it, there is shape.
It looks like nothing and feels like nothing is there.
Yet, in the deepest part of It, there is substance.
It looks like an impenetrable darkness.
Yet, in the deepest part of It, there is clearness and light.
It is the clearest clear and the brightest light!
It has never been forgotten
From the most ancient of ancient days,
Right up to the present moment.

Everything that lives and exists does so because of Tao.
That is a fact!
How can I know that?
They exist and I exist.
Something brought us into existence.
That something is Tao.
So, I know that because I exist, Tao exists.

EVERYONE'S TAO TE CHING

Because Tao exists, I exist.
It's that simple.

CHAPTER 22

You are perfect at being imperfect!
Embrace your imperfection.
That which yields never breaks!
Think about it:
Something must be bent before it is straightened.
Something must be empty before it is filled.
Something must be exhausted before it is refreshed.
There must be less before there can be more.
Too many things are hard to carry –
They weigh you down and slow your pace.

So, wise up!
Cling to Tao!
Be the sermon you would preach!
Don't show off, and you will stand out.
Don't parade yourself, and you will appear regal.
Don't brag about yourself, and you will be applauded.
Be humble, and you will last longer than everyone else.
Nobody in the world can beat you if you don't compete.
If there is no competition, there is no loss or failure.

The ancient saying that says:
"That which yields never breaks" is no empty promise.
Yield and you'll remain intact.
Sway in the wind and you'll persevere.

CHAPTER 23

The Tao of nature does not insist and says very little.
That's why fierce winds don't last all morning.
That's why the sudden downpour can't last all day.

What brings the wind and the rain?
Heaven and earth.
If Heaven and earth can't make anything last forever,
What makes you think that you can?

Pursue Tao and you become a Taoist.
Pursue power and you become powerful.
Pursue failure and you become a failure.

Tao gladly welcomes you when you become a Taoist.
Power gladly welcomes you when you become powerful.
Failure gladly welcomes you when you become a failure.

If you can't trust others,
You'll never be trusted by anyone.

EVERYONE'S TAO TE CHING

CHAPTER 24

You can stand on your tiptoes
And appear taller than others.
But you will be unsteady and easy to knock down.

You can show off to get noticed,
But it isn't your talent that is noticed.

You can parade yourself to be seen,
But you will look foolish when you do.

You can brag about your abilities,
But you will never be praised or respected by anyone else.

Over-estimate your value and put on airs,
And you'll see how fast you're shown the door.

From the point of view of Tao,
Engaging in such excessive behavior
Is like gorging yourself with too much food.
It is a cancerous tumor that grows out of control.
They contribute nothing positive.
They only make you uncomfortable
Or threaten your wellbeing.

If you don't want to be despised,
Then don't behave like that.

EVERYONE'S TAO TE CHING

If you want to get ahead,
Then live Tao.
But you can't do both.

CHAPTER 25

Before anything existed,
Before even heaven and earth,
There was random, chaotic nothingness.
Yet, something was in that chaotic nothingness,
Shaping chaos with order
And clothing nothingness with substance.

It makes no sound.
It has no body.
It is impartial.
It is unchanging.
It never stops working and never gets tired.
You could call It, "The Mother of the World."
I have no idea what Its name is or what to call It,
So, I just call It, "Tao."
If I had to give It a title, I would just call It, "Great."

To be great means to be expansive.
To be expansive is to extend far into the distance.
To extend far into the distance is to have to return.
Tao extends to the farthest distance
And returns to the nearest center.

So, Tao is great.
Heaven is great.
The earth is great.

The ruler is also great.
In the real world, there are four great things,
And the ruler is counted among them.

The earth is the pattern for human beings.
Heaven is the pattern for the earth.
Tao is the pattern for heaven.
And Tao is the pattern for Tao.

CHAPTER 28

Masculine and feminine are understood as opposites.
Embrace both at the same time.
Then you will be like a cavernous ravine –
A natural, protective barrier that nothing can cross.
Then you will find the strength to endure,
And you will become as innocent as a child once more.

White and black are understood as opposites.
Embrace both at the same time.
Then you will be an example for others to follow.
When you are an example for others to follow,
Then you will find the strength to endure.
You'll never lack the strength you need.
There will be no limit to what you can do.

Honor and disgrace are understood as opposites.
Embrace both at the same time.
Then you will be like a fertile valley.
When you are like a fertile valley,
You will have more than enough strength to endure.
You will be like a block of wood
That has never been carved,
Having the potential to be made into anything.

An uncarved block of wood is natural.
It has infinite possibilities.

Carving it does not make it better.
It only makes it different.
Carving the block of wood limits what it is.
It can only be what it has been carved to be.
The uncarved block of wood has infinite possibilities.
Carving it reduces it to a knickknack or a tool.

When the wise are treated like that
Their infinite potential is reduced
And they are made into bureaucrats.
Their expertise is reduced to procedure and red tape.

So, the greatest sculpture of all
Is the one that is never sculpted.

CHAPTER 29

There are those who would take over the world
And bend it to their will.
They always fail.

The world is like a religious object.
It is like a sacred vessel.
It cannot be coerced.
Anyone who tries to coerce it
Only ends up defiling it.
Anyone who tries to seize control of it
Only ends up losing it.

And so,
Some lead and others follow.
Some shout and others whisper.
Some are strong and others are weak.
Some destroy and others are destroyed.

So, wise up!
Avoid extremes.
Avoid excess.
Avoid extravagance.

CHAPTER 30

Make Tao the model for your leadership.
Reject coercion and shows of power or strength.
This only leads to retaliation.
Whatever force you use will be used against you.

Desolation follows armies!
Famine follows battles!
Only thorn bushes grow where soldiers camp.
The food and resources of the land
Are swallowed up by armies.
Nothing is left when they leave.

The best general avoids the fight.
He does what he can to end the battle before it begins.
His strength is not in force but in avoiding conflict.
When conflict cannot be avoided, and he must fight,
He only does what is necessary to win the battle.
He strikes the decisive blow and stops.
He doesn't prolong the battle.
He doesn't expand the battle to others.
He does not boast of his victory when the battle is over.
He simply does what he can to stop the fighting.
His victories do not make him prideful.
He simply does what he can to stop the fighting
Because if he had his way,
He would not have fought at all.

But he was left no choice in the matter.
He simply does what he can do to stop the fighting.
He does not intimidate those he defeated in battle.

Domination and preying on the weak
Goes against Tao.
Whatever goes against Tao
Will come to an untimely end.

CHAPTER 31

As for weapons –

You can design a weapon to be super-sophisticated,
With a fancy name and complicated design specs,
But in the end, it is only a tool for death and destruction.
That's it!
It has no other purpose or use but to kill and destroy.

What else in nature designs and uses weapons?
Nothing!
Everything else in nature finds weapons repugnant.
Everything else refuses to use them.
Those who live Tao refuse to use weapons,
Or even accept their use.

The same man who is peaceful at home
Is violent and ferocious on the battlefield.
Weapons are only instruments of destruction.
They destroy people, the land, the environment,
And also, the humanity of the one who wields them.

If you must fight and if you must use a weapon,
Just do it and don't glorify it.
Your enemies are not monsters!
They are human beings just like you!

EVERYONE'S TAO TE CHING

Is it glorious to take the life of another human being?
Is there glory in war?

Anyone who would glorify war would glorify murder!
Because that is what war is!
Glorifying war is celebrating murder, plain and simple.
Tao can never be with anyone like that.
If you celebrate murder,
You will never get ahead in the world.

When the times are happy,
We honor and celebrate compassion.
When times are sad,
We honor and celebrate violence.
Those going into battle,
Should line themselves up
As if they were lining up at a funeral.
When the battle is over,
Those who survive,
Should weep for the dead on both sides.
The victorious army should not celebrate,
But treat the victory like a funeral.

EVERYONE'S TAO TE CHING

CHAPTER 32

Tao is the eternal nameless name.
It is smaller than the smallest subatomic particle,
And contains the entire universe.

If sovereigns and rulers would cling to Tao,
Then everything would naturally submit to their rule.
Heaven and earth would unite, and sweet dew would fall.
Equality among people would naturally arise
Without the need for laws or governmental programs.

The uncarved block of wood
Has no name before it is sculpted.
Once it is sculpted, whatever it is carved into
Is given a name or a label.
We know them by their names,
But their names limit their potential.
They limit what they are and what they can be.
Use the name to identify,
But don't use the name to limit.
Limit your need to limit others!
Tao has no limits and limits nothing.
Tao flows in and through the world,
And does not care about names or labels
Any more than the stream and rivers
Care about which ocean or sea they flow into.

CHAPTER 33

Understand others, and you'll be clever.
Understand yourself, and you'll be wise.
Conquer others, and you'll be strong.
Conquer yourself, and you'll be powerful.
Know that you have enough, and you'll be rich.
Be determined and you'll have direction.
Stand your ground and you'll persevere.
Live your life!
Don't just witness it or sleepwalk through it.
Make the reality of your death a part of your life,
And the moment will be filled with immortality.

CHAPTER 34

Tao is far-reaching,
Extending in every direction.
It extends left and right and up and down and in and out.

Everything that is alive depends on Tao for life.
And yet, Tao doesn't claim authority or rule over them.
Tao accomplishes everything it sets out to do.
And yet, Tao is anonymous.
Everything that exists is clothed and nurtured by Tao.
And yet, Tao doesn't bully or coerce anything.

Tao appears insignificant
Because it doesn't have any wants or desires.
You can call it "Great"
Because it is not a tyrant
And doesn't bully or coerce anything
That commits its life to Tao.
Tao is great because it does not strive for greatness.

CHAPTER 35

Embrace the great image of Tao
And the whole world will beat a path to your door.
Wherever you go, you'll always be safe
Because everything will be at peace from your presence.

People on a stroll will always stop
To listen to music or to taste samples of food.
But they don't stop for Tao
Because Tao has no flavor and there is nothing to taste.
Tao makes no sound so there is nothing to hear.
Tao cannot be seen or heard
And Its supply can never be exhausted.

CHAPTER 36

Something must be larger before it can be shrunken.
Something must be stronger before it can be weakened.
Something must be set up before it can be knocked over.
Something must have before it can be taken away.

The wisdom hidden in plain sight
Is that whatever is yielding and weak
Conquers what is rigid and strong.

A fish can't live if it is taken out of the water.
A government can't survive if its secrets are revealed.

CHAPTER 37

Tao never acts.
Yet, everything is done.

When sovereigns and rulers cling to Tao,
Then all things are naturally transformed.
Should desire raise its ugly head once more,
I would simply clobber it
With a nameless, uncarved block of wood.
The uncarved block of wood is simplicity
And freedom from desires.
Abandon desire and embrace simplicity.
That is how you cultivate serenity.
When you cultivate serenity in yourself,
The whole world will naturally be at peace.

EVERYONE'S TAO TE CHING

THE BOOK OF POWER

CHAPTER 38

You only get to keep it by giving it away.
That is the secret of power.
The virtuous person is unaware of his virtue.
The truly powerful never seek to hold onto power.
They become powerful by sharing power with others.
That's why they are powerful.

Those who strive for power,
Trying to hold onto power and keep it for themselves,
Are not truly powerful.
They simply think they have power.
If they had power, they would share it.
Since they don't share it, they don't have it.

If you have true power,
Then you will never act, never force,
And everything gets done.
If you only think you have power,
You constantly act, constantly force,
And things never get finished.

Those who are truly compassionate
Are compassion in action.
When they act, they exude compassion,

Not because it is right
Not because they expect to receive reward or honor,
Not because they expect any kind of gain,
But simply because they are filled with compassion
And it flows out of them.

Those who are truly moral
Are morality in action.
When they act, they exude morality,
Not because it is right,
Not because they expect to receive reward or honor,
Not because they expect any kind of gain,
But simply because they are filled with morality
And it flows out of them.

Those who are righteous and pious
Are righteous and pious in their actions.
But if nobody acknowledges it,
They get angry.
They roll up their sleeves
And get to work imposing
A system of righteousness and piety on everyone else.

Remember Tao and it all works out.
Forget Tao,
And you will strive for power.
Forget power,
And you will strive for compassion.

Forget compassion,
And you will strive for righteousness.
Forget righteousness,
And you will strive for rituals and tradition.
In the end,
The rituals and tradition will be all there is.
You'll forget why you have them in the first place,
And you will become a slave to the rules.
Rituals and tradition are the husk of faith,
But not the faith itself.
In the end, it falls apart
And what you hoped to preserve will be lost.
You think you are serving Tao
But you are merely serving your own sense of order.

If you want to be great
Focus on the substance, not on the surface.
Seek the fruit and not the flower.
Live so that everybody gains, and no one loses.
Celebrate when you are paid, not when you are promised.
Live in the reality of how it is,
Not in the fantasy of how you want it
Or how you think it should be.

CHAPTER 39

Oneness with Tao is achievable.
It has happened in the past.
Heaven becoming one with Tao
Became clear and expansive.
The earth becoming one with Tao
Became solid and firm.
Spirits becoming one with Tao
Became gods.
Valleys becoming one with Tao
Became fertile and lush.
Creation becoming one with Tao
Erupted with life.
Powerful men becoming one with Tao
Became rulers of Empires and kings of nations.

Everything is what it is because of Tao.
Heaven losing oneness with Tao,
Would shatter and fall.
The earth losing oneness with Tao,
Would crumble and fall away.
Spirits losing oneness with Tao
Would disperse and cease to exist.
Valleys losing oneness with Tao
Would become barren wastelands.
Creation losing oneness with Tao
Would cause all life to go extinct.

Emperors and kings losing oneness with Tao
Would be overthrown.

Humility must be the foundation of greatness.
Just as what is low is the foundation for what is high.
Successful emperors and kings of old knew this,
Styling themselves as abandoned, undeserving, and poor.
They denigrated themselves
So that others would praise them.
After all, too much honor
Is often no honor at all,
And thinking too much of yourself
Often makes others think less of you.

Don't just look at the showy and the superficial.
Focus instead on the dull substance.
Don't look for the glitter of jewels,
But look for the durability of stone.

CHAPTER 40

Tao advances by retreating.
The strength of Tao is in yielding.
Everything that exists was born of something that exists.
Yet, there was a time when what exists had no existence.
What is was born from what was not.
Something was born from nothing.

CHAPTER 41

When those who are wise learn about Tao,
They diligently attempt to apply It to their lives.
When those who are average learn about Tao,
They apply some of It and ignore the rest of it.
When those who are stupid learn about Tao,
They laugh out loud.
If stupid people didn't laugh at It,
Then It wouldn't be Tao.

That's why the old saying goes:
The path to light appears dark.
The path that leads forward appears like a U-turn.
The smoothest path appears uneven and rocky.
Truest power appears weak.
The purest white appears smudged.
The highest good appears insufficient.
The deepest commitment appears fickle.
The most constant appears changeable.
The squarest square has no corners.
The best keepsake takes time to make.
The highest tone is inaudible.
The greatest image has no shape.

Tao is everywhere and nowhere to be found.
You can't see it.
You can't call it by name.

You can't make it appear on command.
Yet Tao alone nurtures all that is
And brings them to their destination.

CHAPTER 42

Tao gave birth to unity.
Then unity gave birth to Yin and Yang.
Yin and Yang gave birth to the life force.
The life force gave birth to all living things.
Everything that exists carries Yin on its back
While holding Yang in its arms.
The intermingling of Yin and Yang
Produces a state of harmony.

There are no more hated words
Than "abandoned," "undeserving," and "poor."
Yet, that is how emperors and kings refer to themselves.
Sometimes in life you gain more by losing,
And you lose more by gaining.

I also teach what others have taught:
Those who are violent will not live long, happy lives,
Neither will they die from natural causes.
That is the core of what I teach.

CHAPTER 43

That which yields the most
Overpowers that which is the most rigid.
That which has no substance
Can penetrate that which has no opening.
That is why I know that it is often best to do nothing.

There are very few people alive in the world today
Who can understand the benefit
Of teaching others without words,
Of taking no action and going with the flow.

CHAPTER 44

What is more important to you,
Fame or well-being?
What is worth more to you,
Your well-being or your wealth?
What is more harmful to you,
Success or failure?

Greed is expensive —
Wanting something only increases its price.

You can't lose what you don't have.
But if you have a lot, you will end up losing a lot.
You'll never be humiliated
If you are content with what you have.
You'll never be in danger
If you know your limits.
That's how to endure for a long time.

CHAPTER 45

The best outcome may look like a mistake in the moment,
But the good that results from it continues.
Complete fullness may look empty,
But when you draw from it, it never runs dry.
The straightest object may look bent.
The most skilled person may look clumsy and inept.
The most eloquent speech may sound awkward.

Move around to warm yourself when you are cold.
Be as still as possible to cool yourself when you are hot.
But hot or cold, be at peace.
Always remain quiet and tranquil,
And the world will be yours.

CHAPTER 46

Whenever a nation lives Tao,
Its strongest and swiftest horses
Are used to plow and fertilize farmers' fields.

Whenever a nation does not live Tao,
Its strongest and swiftest horses
Are used to wage war against its neighbors.

Wanting more than you need is a crime.
No crime is worse!
Not being satisfied with what you have is a disaster.
No disaster is worse!
Being greedy is a misfortune.
No misfortune is worse!

Know that you have enough,
And you'll always have enough.

CHAPTER 47

You can know what is happening in the world
Without ever leaving your house.
You can see the Tao of heaven
Without ever peering out of your window.
The more you travel,
The less sure you are about your assumptions.
Wise up!
Have the mind of a traveler
Without going anywhere.
Be open to how others live.
Use your intuition to know what is going on.
Accomplish things by not forcing anything,
But by going with the flow and letting events play out.

CHAPTER 48

To be educated,
You must learn more and more each day.
To become Tao,
You must unlearn more and more each day.
Unlearn more and more each day
Until you realize that you do not have to do anything
For everything to be done.
By not forcing your will on the situation,
The situation naturally works itself out.

Things have a way of sorting themselves out
If you stop trying to force them.
You can win the whole world
If only you stop trying to own it.
But if you attempt to own the world,
Then you are not worthy of having it.

CHAPTER 49

Wise up!
Don't have a closed mind.
Always be willing to listen to different points of view.

I'm good to those who are good to me.
I'm good to those who are not good to me.
By doing so, I show the power of goodness
And goodness is increased.

I trust those who are trustworthy.
I trust those who are untrustworthy.
By doing so, I show the power of trust
And trust is increased.

Wise up!
Don't rock the boat!
Don't stir up conflicts or disagreements!
Be at peace with everyone.
Treat everyone the same.
Because there is no guile in what you do or say,
You will be as unthreatening as a child.
And since you are no threat to them,
They will pay attention to you
And listen to what you have to say.

EVERYONE'S TAO TE CHING

CHAPTER 50

All that is born to life is born to die.
The road of life only leads to one destination.

Three out of ten people will live to a ripe, old age.
Three out of ten people will die prematurely.
Three out of ten people will burn through life too soon.
Why?
Because they set out to "seize the day,"
But they only seize their deaths through reckless living.

But there are one out of ten who know how to live.
They are visitors in life and do not provoke death
By claiming ownership of life or permanence.
Rumors about these people say that they can travel
Without ever running into a rhinoceros or a tiger.
The rumors say that they can stand up to an entire army
Without being harmed at all.
Rumors say that if they were to run across a rhinoceros,
It wouldn't be able to gouge them with its horn.
If they were to run across a tiger,
It wouldn't be able to maul them with its claws.
If they were to stand up to an entire army,
Nothing would be able to kill them or even wound them.

"Get real!" You say.
"How is any of that possible?" you ask.

It's simple:

By embracing death, you embrace life.

Embracing your mortality makes you alive.

When you are full of life,

There is no room in you for death.

CHAPTER 51

Everything that lives is a manifestation of Tao.
Everything is empowered and nurtured by Tao.
Everything is given shape and substance by Tao.
Everything is placed in an environment and a context,
Allowing it to develop and giving it room to grow.

So, everything honors Tao whether they know it or not.
They honor Tao and respect Its power.
They don't do this because they are commanded to do so.
They do it simply because it is natural for them to do it.

Tao gives them life.
Tao gives them nourishment.
Tao mothers them and provides for them.
Tao matures them.
Tao protects them.

Tao gives them life,
But Tao doesn't claim to own them.
Tao assists them,
But Tao doesn't demand gratitude from them.
Tao is their protector,
But Tao doesn't lord it over them.
That's why Tao is impossible to understand –
It is a force that does not force.

EVERYONE'S TAO TE CHING

CHAPTER 52

Something is responsible
For the creation of the world.
Whatever that something is,
It can be considered the Mother of the World.

You can get to know the Mother
By getting to know Her children.
Once you have known Her children,
You can return to the Mother,
Knowing Her even better than before.

Knowing the Mother
Is like becoming one of Her own children.
She will nourish you and protect you
For the rest of your life.

Open your mind and close your mouth!
Lock up your ego!
You will remain beyond trouble.
Close your mind and open your mouth.
Set your ego free.
You will remain beyond help.

When you notice the little things
They say you are perceptive.
When you are flexible

EVERYONE'S TAO TE CHING

They say you are unbreakable.
Don't focus on the faults of others,
But shine a light on your own failings.
Search out your own blind spots and inflexibility.
Don't be the cause of your own undoing!
The way to avoid inviting disaster upon yourself
Is to pursue and practice perseverance.

CHAPTER 53

Living Tao is like traveling down a highway.
My only fear would be taking the wrong exit
And finding myself in a place
Where I couldn't find the highway again.
Because that is what Tao is like!
It is like a smooth, level highway.
Yet people prefer to take
Pothole-ridden, uneven back roads.

The courts of the powerful only yield corruption,
While the fields of the poor only yield weeds.
The palaces of the wealthy are filled with riches,
While the granaries of the poor are filled with nothing.
There isn't enough food and supplies to go around,
But the rich have more than they could ever need.
The greater the imbalance between rich and poor,
The more the poor suffer at the hands of the rich.
The more the rich gain,
The more the poor lose.

As the poor starve,
The rich spend their money on expensive clothing.
They adorn themselves with extravagant jewelry.
They gorge themselves with too much food
And they drink too much wine.

They hoard more and more
And the people have less and less.

You can give it some fancy economic label if you want to.
You can call it "trickle-down" or "Laissez-faire,"
But I will call it what it is:
Robbing from the poor to give to the rich.
That's it!
Plain and simple!
It's stealing and nothing else!
The rich are no better than thieves!
They are no better than gangsters!
The government that serves them is organized crime!

They abuse Tao by abusing others.
They know nothing of Tao
And only know suffering –
How to cause it for others,
And how to invite it upon themselves.

CHAPTER 54

If the roots are deep,
It cannot be pulled up.
A tight embrace,
Cannot be pushed away.
What a family is like in one generation
Will be repeated generation after generation.

Let your roots dig deep into Tao!
Embrace Tao as tightly as you can!
If you do,
You will have genuine power.
If your family does,
Generational cycles will be broken
And your family will become prominent in your town.
If your town does,
It will become an important cultural center in the nation.
If your nation does,
It will become powerful in world affairs.
If the world does,
Everyone will be empowered.

Don't judge your insides
By looking at other peoples' outsides.
Don't judge yourself by how you think you should be.
Look at yourself through the context of yourself.
Don't judge a family by how you think it should be.

Look at the family through the context of the family.
Don't judge a town by how you think it should be.
Look at the town through the context of the town.
Don't judge a nation by how you think it should be.
Look at a nation through the context of the nation.
Don't judge the world by how you think it should be.
Judge the world through the context of the world.
If you want to know what the world is really like,
Let the world be the world as it is.
That's how I know what the world is like
And how I have learned to know myself.

CHAPTER 55

Anyone who possesses an abundance of power
Is like a newborn baby
That the wasps and scorpions can't sting,
The ferocious animals can't attack,
Or large birds of prey can't carry off.
He is weak,
Yet he can grasp a finger tightly.
He has no sexual desire,
Yet he has enough virility for an erection.
He can wail and cry all day
And never become hoarse or lose his voice.
He can do this because he is in harmony with himself.
That harmony produces balance.

When you know that harmony and balance,
You'll experience what is eternal.
When you experience what is eternal,
You'll know enlightenment.

An empty life is a full life.
Seeking to empty your life invites blessing.
Seeking to advance your life invites bad luck.
Seeking to be the master of your own destiny
And to impose your will is violence.
Trying to control what is out of your control
Results in tumultuous calamity.

If you are truly strong,
You'll never intimidate anyone weaker than you.
To do so would be to go against Tao.
Anyone who goes against Tao
Will come to an untimely end.

EVERYONE'S TAO TE CHING

CHAPTER 56

Understanding is silent.
Ignorance and indifference never shut up.
If you want to know,
You'll keep from talking.
If you want to talk,
You'll keep from knowing.

Shut up!
Keep quiet!
Still your tongue!
Let go of your need to be right!
Put a lid on your smug intellect!
Stop wandering down the worn-out path of certainty,
But travel down the unfamiliar road of not knowing.

You're like an agitated cloud of dust.
Your words, desires, thoughts, actions, all of it
Keeps the dust forever moving around
In a suspended haze of ego.
Be still and silent and let the dust settle.
Make peace with the stillness.
Make peace with the dust
And the dust will settle and be at rest.
You'll find a sense of profound oneness with everything.
You'll find your true self.

In that profound sense of oneness
Where you find your true self,
You'll see that there is no friend or enemy,
There is no winning or losing,
There is no honor or disgrace,
It's all one in the same
And you are one with it all.
Then you'll be valued beyond measure.

CHAPTER 57

Govern the nation with honesty
And by observing customs and procedure.
Wage war with deception
And the element of surprise.
Rule the world by leaving it alone
And not interfering with it.

How do I know that?
Because I have eyes and I have seen
That more laws and regulations
Only lead to more poverty for the people.
More weapons available to everyone,
Only makes everyone more unsafe.
The shrewder people try to be,
The more bizarre the schemes become.
Every new law that is passed
Creates an outlaw who didn't exist before.

Wise up!
Leaders used to say things like:
"If I keep from meddling with peoples' lives,
The people reform themselves."
"If I remain silent and stop being self-righteous,
The people end up doing what is right on their own."
"If I keep from meddling in the peoples' livelihoods,
The people become prosperous on their own."

"If I let go of my expectation of what the people should be,
They begin to express limitless potential
In ways I could never have envisioned for them.
They are like an uncarved block of wood
That can become anything before it is carved.

CHAPTER 58

If the government doesn't meddle in peoples' lives,
The people remain content and honest.
If the government meddles in their lives,
The people become devious and crafty.

Good luck rests on bad luck.
Bad luck hides behind good luck.
In the end, who can say what is good or bad?
It's a riddle.
All simple truths dissolve into riddles.
What looks good today may turn out to be bad.
What looks bad tomorrow may turn out to be good.
Do you think we are the first to be puzzled by this?
People have always been perplexed by it.

Wise up!
Be firm, but not harsh.
Be serious, but not severe.
Be honest, but not brutally so.
Shine brightly but do not blind.

CHAPTER 59

Moderation is key.
There's nothing better!
Practice moderation when leading.
Practice moderation when following and serving.
Commitment to Tao
Resides in avoiding the "either/or" of extremes,
And dwelling in the "both/and" of moderation.

Power flows out from you when you live Tao.
When that happens,
You can do anything.
When you can do anything,
You'll be unstoppable.
When you are unstoppable,
Your power will be beyond measure.
When your power is beyond measure,
Then you'll be fit to govern others.

Govern others like a mother raises her children.
You'll dig deep roots and establish a firm foundation.

That's how to have a full and long life.

CHAPTER 60

Governing a large nation
Is like cooking a small fish.
Too much attention and it falls apart.

Model yourself on Tao
And you will not be troubled by the past.
The past will have no sway over you.
The past will still be the past.
It will still have its hurts and traumas,
But you will stop defining yourself
By what has happened to you.
You will no longer be haunted, but whole.

You'll also see through fast-talking con men
And smooth-talking politicians.
You'll see who is sincere and wise,
And who are the predators
That wear a disguise of sincerity and wisdom.

When the past no longer haunts you
And con men and politicians can no longer fool you,
You will then find the power to be free.

CHAPTER 61

A large nation is like a river
Flowing through a deep valley.
The river has been formed
By the joining together
Of all the rivers and streams
Running through the mountains.
Just as a woman receives a man in the act of love,
The river is receptive and open.
The woman conquers the man
By receiving him into herself.
That is what the river is like,
Open, receptive, conquering,
By deliberately taking the lowest position.

So, if a large nation is receptive,
It eventually incorporates a smaller nation into itself.
If a small nation is receptive,
It eventually becomes the ruler of a large nation.
So, one nation becomes the ruler of the other
Because it is receptive.
One nation becomes ruled by the other,
Because it is not.

The large nation wants to annex the small nation.
The small nation wants to have influence
In the affairs of the large nation.

If the large nation governs in such a way
That it serves the needs of the small nation,
Then both nations get what they want.

CHAPTER 62

Tao is a mystery to everything.
To the good man, it is a treasure.
To the bad man it is a refuge.

Words are cheap.
Yet flattery wins favor.
Hollow gestures are empty.
Yet they can get you noticed.
Don't abandon the scoundrel and the flatterer,
But show them the way of Tao.

When a ruler is chosen and officials are appointed,
You can serve him with your wealth,
By making grand gestures,
And by your sycophantic behavior.
You can be a yes-man and a brown-noser.
But if you really want to serve the ruler,
Give him the gift of Tao.
If you offer Tao to the ruler,
You will be worth more
Than all the "yes-men" and "brown-nosers" put together.

Why was Tao so highly valued in the past?
Because with Tao, everybody wins.
With Tao, you will find what you seek.
With Tao, your mistakes will be corrected,

And you will receive forgiveness.
That's why Tao is so highly valued by all.

CHAPTER 63

Go with the flow.
Act, but don't meddle.
Find flavor in what is tasteless.
Treat the insignificant as though they are important.
Treat the minority as though they were the majority.
Be kind to those who wrong you.

Resolve difficulties while they are still easy.
Attend to big things while they are still small.
The most difficult tasks in the world
Begin as things that are easy.
The greatest things in the world
Begin as things that are unimportant.
Wise up!
Don't strive for greatness.
Then you will succeed in becoming great.

Rash promises are rarely kept.
Don't trust them.
If you think everything should be easy
You'll experience a lot of hardships.
Wise up!
There are a lot of difficulties and hardships.
Accept it.
And nothing will be too difficult or hard for you.

CHAPTER 64

It's easy to restrain what isn't moving.
Plans seem easy to accomplish before you begin.
It's easy to shatter what is brittle.
It's easy to disperse minute particles.
Solve the problem before it arises.
Order things before they become chaotic.

A tree can grow so large
That a man can't put his arms around it.
Yet, that giant tree began as a tiny seed.
The largest building begins as a single shovelful of dirt.
A journey of a thousand miles begins with a single step.

If you meddle in things,
You will ruin them.
If you try to hold onto things,
You will lose them.
Wise up!
Don't meddle, and nothing will be ruined.
Don't hold on to things, and nothing will be lost.

People often ruin what they are working on
Just as they are on the verge of completing it.
So, be just as careful when finishing tasks
As you are when you are beginning them.
Then you'll never ruin anything.

EVERYONE'S TAO TE CHING

Wise up!
Minimize your wants.
Don't value rare items.
Unlearn everything you have learned.
Let everything and everyone be what it is.
Go with the flow.

CHAPTER 65

People who lived Tao long ago
Did not give the people too much to think about.
They only gave people what they needed to know.
People are too difficult to govern
When they have too much to think about.
They can't be taught anything
When they already think they know it all.
You can't convince them with facts
When their minds are already made up.

The nation suffers when leaders are clever.
The nation prospers when the leader is honest.
Always remember that!
If you understand that,
You will be powerful in a way no one understands.

That sort of power digs deep and is far reaching.
It is adaptable.
It keeps everything from running off in their own direction
And brings them back into harmony.
And everything becomes one.

CHAPTER 66

Large rivers and oceans are larger and grander
Than all the valleys and streams.
There's a simple reason for why this is so.
Large rivers and oceans take the lowest position.

If you want to be in charge
Speak humbly to everyone.
If you want to lead,
You must learn how to follow.

Wise up!
If you lead this way,
People will carry you on their shoulders
And you'll never be too heavy for them to hold up.
They'll never get tired.
You can stand in front of the people
And they will not see you as being in the way.
Everyone will applaud your leadership
And you will have their undying support.

If you never compete with anything,
Nothing can ever compete with you.

CHAPTER 67

People everywhere call me an idiot
And say that what I teach is stupid.
They say my views on Tao have no practical value
And do not reflect the real world.
That's what makes it Tao!
It is infinite and unique.
That's what makes Tao great!
If it were like everything else,
It wouldn't be great.
It would be small, narrow, and insignificant.

In life, I value three things.
They are the three treasures I hold dear.
First, I have compassion.
Second, I practice moderation.
Third, I seek humility and don't need to be first.

Because I have compassion, I have no fear.
Because I practice moderation, I have no lack.
Because I seek humility and don't need to be first,
I have room to grow and my influence increases.

Don't be like people today.
They try to be fearless without compassion,
Which only makes them vicious.
They try to avoid lack without practicing moderation,

Which only makes them self-indulgent.
They seek influence and being first without humility,
Which is essentially a death sentence.

Compassion is your shield!
Take it with you when you find yourself in conflict
And you'll emerge victorious.
Nothing can harm you.
If you are attacked, compassion will defend you.
Heaven protects those who have compassion.

CHAPTER 68

The superior warrior avoids fighting.
The superior fighter avoids anger.
The superior conqueror avoids battles.
The superior leader avoids force,
But is open to the views of others.

There is great power in not contending.
Everyone has their own strengths.
Help them to develop them.
You'll mirror the Tao of heaven
And embody the wisdom of the ancients.

CHAPTER 69

The strategists use to say:
"Don't make the first move,
But let the other take the initiative."
"Don't start a fight.
Let the other start it."
"Don't take an inch,
But retreat a yard."

You can call this moving forward without advancing.
It is showing your strength without resorting to violence.
It is taking prisoners without vanquishing.
It is using the weapon of having no weapons.

The worst mistake you can make
Is rushing out to fight an enemy.
It is disastrous!
You can't win,
And in the process,
You'll lose your compassion, moderation, and humility –
The Three Treasures you should hold dear.
And so, whenever two armies are arranged for battle,
It is the army that regrets going to war that wins.

EVERYONE'S TAO TE CHING

CHAPTER 70

No one is too dumb to know Tao
But many are too smart.
I speak simple words and perform simple actions.
But you are too clever to understand them.
You are too smart to do them.
But my words are not my own.
They come from an ancient source.
My deeds are governed by that source.
If you understood that source,
You would understand me.
But since you don't, you won't.
Very few people get where I'm coming from.
Those who ridicule me and mistreat me are praised.

Wise up!
Be like the wise man
Who wears coarse, itchy robes
While carrying a priceless jewel
Concealed in the inside pocket next to his heart.
He may look austere and uncomfortable on the outside,
But on the inside, he is content and at peace.
So, live simply and you'll find a treasure
That is impossible to steal.

CHAPTER 71

I don't care how smart you are,
You don't know everything.
Remember that!
Knowing that you don't know is healthy.
Not knowing that you don't know is a tragic illness.
Seek the cure!
But you can't be cured if you refuse to accept you are sick.

Wise up!
When you're sick and tired of being sick and tired,
You'll be on the path to healing.
When you stop being an expert
In matters you know nothing about,
You'll be healthy.
Know the symptoms of your disease,
And your dis-ease will transform into ease.

CHAPTER 72

The dread of authoritarianism
Preserves freedom for everyone.
When people lose that dread,
They wake up one morning to discover
They are living in a dictatorship.

If you want to keep the people content,
If you want to avoid rebellion,
Then don't interfere with their home life.
Don't interfere with their livelihoods.
Don't impose a lot of rules and laws and customs.
Don't meddle and leave them alone as much as possible
And they will give you their undying loyalty.

Wise up!
Know yourself, but don't show yourself!
Upgrade yourself, but don't parade yourself!
Don't fault yourself, but don't exalt yourself!
Let go of your need to be praised and honored
So that you can act in a way that is praised and honored.

CHAPTER 73

You can have a short, turbulent life seeking glory,
Or you can have a long, peaceful life seeking anonymity.
Be heroic at being bold, and you'll find an early grave.
Be heroic at being meek, and you'll find a long life.
It's that simple.
One path leads to safety.
The other leads to destruction.
Which do you want for yourself?

Heaven likes what it likes and hates what it hates.
Who knows why?
Even the very wise are at a loss to explain it.

The Tao of heaven always wins, but It never competes.
It always answers, but It never speaks.
It is always inviting, but It never summons or compels.
Everything comes to It naturally on their own.
It is always planning and involved in the details,
Even though It appears to be inattentive.

Heaven is a large net and the holes in its mesh are wide.
Even so, nothing ever slips through those holes.
Nothing is ever lost.

CHAPTER 74

If people aren't afraid of dying,
How could you threaten them with death?
If people are afraid of dying,
And if you gathered up all the rabble-rousers
And threaten them with the death penalty,
Who would stir up trouble?

If you are doling out life and death,
You are in over your head.
You have no idea what you are doing.
There's only one
who knows how to give life and bring death.
That one is Tao.
Tao is a Master Executioner,
Knowing how to execute correctly and justly.
Rulers and governments who execute people
Are overstepping their authority and skill.
They replace Tao with their own desire
And people suffer.
It's like some guy off the street
Replacing a master carpenter building a house,
Thinking he knows how to build as well as the carpenter,
Thinking he knows how to use the equipment just as well,
But what happens?
He makes a mess of things
And hurts himself in the process.

Instead of building a house,
He only creates a pile of rubble
And is lucky if he doesn't cut off his own hands.

CHAPTER 75

People are starving!
Why are they starving?
Because taxes eat the grain
And the people eat nothing.
So, the people starve.

The people are rebellious.
Why are they rebellious?
Because rulers meddle in their lives too much
And eat their freedom.
So, the people are rebellious.

The people believe that life is pointless.
Why do they believe life is pointless?
Because the rich and powerful take more and more
And the people have less and less,
And life becomes reduced to merely surviving.
So, the people believe that life is pointless.

Ironically,
Those who have been robbed of everything
Are often the only ones who can see things clearly.
Ironically,
Those who have lost all sense of meaning or purpose
Are often the only ones who find meaning and purpose.

CHAPTER 76

People are born soft and flexible.
They die hard and rigid.
Everything that lives,
Even the grass and trees,
Are soft and flexible while alive,
But they are dried out and shriveled when dead.

So, think of it this way:
Those who are rigid and inflexible
Are friends with death –
They are death's traveling companions.
Those who are adaptable and flexible
Are friends with life –
They are life's traveling companions.

Therefore, an inflexible strategy cannot win.
A tree that grows too large and strong is chopped down.
Those who try to hold onto power lose it.
The bigger they are the harder they fall.
Each of these will be replaced
By whatever and whoever is adaptable and flexible.

CHAPTER 77

The Tao of heaven
Is like pulling the string of a bow.
The upper part of the bow bends down.
The lower part of the bow bends up.
In a way, you can say
That something is taken from the top
And added to the bottom.
So, just like the bow
The Tao of heaven removes extremes
And moves toward the center.
The Tao of heaven
Is to take from what has too much
And give it to what doesn't have enough.

But what do people do?
They shun the center
And to rush to the extremes.
They take from what doesn't have enough
And gives it to what has too much.

Who can live with excess,
And not use it to indulge themselves and their desires,
But instead, use it to supply the needs
Of those who don't have enough?
Only those who live Tao.
No one else can.

Wise up!
Help those who need help,
But don't demand gratitude for what you do.
Do what must be done,
But don't seek credit for it.
You can only do that
If you don't consider yourself
To be more worthy than anyone else.

CHAPTER 78

There is nothing in the entire world like water!

Water yields more than anything else.
It embraces weakness.
Because of this,
You could be the strongest person in the world
And you couldn't punch a hole in the water.
You wouldn't even be able to dent it.
With all your strength,
You would never be able to push back a flood.
To do any of that,
You would need to use something weaker than water.
And there is nothing weaker than water.
There is nothing more yielding.

Water is soft and yielding.
Yet, it wears away the hardest stone
And carries away the firmest earth.

That which is adaptable
Always triumphs over that which is inflexible.
That which is yielding
Always triumphs over that which is rigid.
People all over the world instinctively seem to know this.
And yet, no one seems to live by it.
They never seem to put it into practice.

Wise up!
They used to say that if you accept responsibility,
Then you can solve the problem.

A good leader accepts responsibility
And because he does that,
He can fix whatever problems the nation endures
And all the people become prosperous.
Because he accepts the responsibility for all the problems,
He can become the ruler of the world.

Sincere truth defies common sense.
Honest words come as a paradox.

CHAPTER 79

When longstanding adversaries
Finally make peace with each other,
There is bound to be a lot of lingering resentment.
So how can this be called being "at peace"?
And how can peace be truly achieved?

It's like when one person owes another person money.
The one who owes
Is in the power of the one who loans.
The one who loans
Loses more and more power over the debtor
As the loan is repaid.
And it doesn't matter how grateful
The debtor was to receive the loan in the first place,
He loses his gratitude as he pays the loan.
He grumbles against the person who gave the loan,
Just like he complains about paying taxes.

So, be like someone who loans money
But never demands repayment.

That is the Tao of heaven!
Heaven shows no favoritism.
It doesn't value one person over another.
It often seems like it's working
For the benefit of the good person,

But that is simply because
The good person is working
In harmony with the Tao of heaven.

EVERYONE'S TAO TE CHING

CHAPTER 80

A large nation with a large population
Always sets out to explore
For new lands and new resources.
They forge weapons and conquer others.
So, a large population creates conquest and suffering
At home and abroad.

So, the ideal nation is small with few people.
There may be enough weapons to go around,
But those weapons are never used.
They have enough of life
That they do not rush off
To cause death for others or risk death for themselves.
They will not explore new lands to conquer
Or seek out new lands to settle.
They will be content to stay where they are.
Even if there are more than enough transports,
Even if there are more than enough battleships,
Even if there is more than enough armor to go around,
Even if there are more than enough weapons,
The people will never use them.

If they are content,
They will look after their own affairs
And maintain their own sense of independence.
As a result,

Their food will have more flavor.
Their clothes will appear more luxurious.
Their homes will seem grander.
They will feel safer and more secure.
They will be happy with their quality of life.

Even if the nation borders on another so closely
That the people of the other nation can be seen,
And the sounds of barking dogs
And crowing roosters can be heard,
The people of that nation will never visit the other.
They will grow old and die at home
And never be curious about what the other nation is like
Because they are happy and content where they are.

CHAPTER 81

Sincere words don't flatter.
flattering words are not sincere.
The one who knows doesn't argue.
The one who argues doesn't know.
Those who are wise don't think they know a lot.
Those who think they know a lot are not wise.

Wise up!
Don't hoard anything.
The more you give to others,
The more you will ultimately have.
If you were to give everything you have to others,
You would find true wealth and be the richest man alive.

That's the Tao of heaven!
It always lends a helping hand
And never causes any harm.
That's the Tao of the wise!
They are always willing to lend a helping hand
And never compete with anyone or anything.

INDEX

accept, 10, 49, 72, 129, 138
agree with you, 54
ambition, 25, 42, 55
argue, 30, 144
armies, 70, 127
army, 73, 97, 127
authoritarianism, 130
authority, 10, 11, 37, 76, 132
bad, 14, 23, 25, 34, 54, 66, 106, 112, 117
battle, 70, 71, 72, 73, 126, 127
compassion, 16, 17, 53, 73, 81, 82, 83, 124, 125, 127
compete, 33, 59, 123, 144
conquer, 65, 75, 78, 115, 142
content, 91, 112, 128, 130, 142, 143
country, 42, 43, 65
death, 29, 48, 72, 75, 97, 98, 125, 132, 135, 142
dictatorship, 130
die, 89, 97, 135, 143
disgrace, 41, 67, 109

earth, 15, 21, 29, 31, 32, 60, 63, 64, 74, 84, 138
ego, 17, 100, 108
empty, 15, 27, 29, 31, 34, 38, 48, 59, 92, 106, 117
empty yourself, 47, 48
enemy, 30, 72, 109, 127
Eternal Mother, 31
excess, 17, 18, 69, 136
extremes, 17, 18, 30, 69, 113, 136
faith, 83
fame, 91
fate, 48
favor, 25, 41, 117
favoritism, 25, 29, 140
fear, 32, 41, 54, 102, 124
fighting, 70, 71, 126
flexible, 100, 135
follow, 23, 51, 67, 69, 70, 113, 123
force, 15, 16, 70, 81, 89, 95, 99, 126
freedom, 36, 79, 130, 134
gain, 42, 53, 82, 89, 102
Get out of your head, 21, 44, 53

Go with the flow, 15, 23, 26, 90, 94, 119, 121
good, 5, 6, 12, 14, 23, 25, 26, 33, 34, 54, 66, 87, 92, 96, 112, 117, 139, 140, 141
govern, 26, 42, 52, 113, 122
governing, 42
greed, 25, 91
heaven, 21, 29, 31, 32, 34, 49, 60, 63, 64, 74, 84, 94, 125, 126, 131, 136, 140, 141, 144
honest, 112, 122, 139
honesty, 110
honor, 29, 67, 73, 82, 85, 99, 109
humility, 16, 17, 25, 85, 124, 125, 127
immortality, 75
impermanence, 27, 36, 60
Indescribable Mother, 31
inflexible, 101, 135, 138
interfere, 110, 130
leader, 25, 26, 50, 65, 122, 126, 139
life, 9, 15, 17, 31, 37, 42, 49, 54, 73, 75, 76, 84, 89, 97, 98, 99, 100, 106, 113, 124, 130, 131, 132, 134, 135, 142, 143
livelihoods, 110, 130
lowest position, 33, 115, 123
luck, 34, 106, 112
 bad luck, 34, 49, 93, 112
 good luck, 112
meddle, 50, 112, 119, 120, 130, 134
moderation, 16, 17, 113, 124, 127
moral, 14, 82
morality, 11, 82
Mother of the World, 56, 63, 100
nation, 42, 52, 53, 93, 104, 105, 110, 114, 115, 116, 122, 139, 142, 143
opinion, 30
parade yourself, 59, 61, 130
paradox, 22, 139
peace, 42, 55, 72, 77, 79, 92, 96, 108, 128, 140
permanent, 34
pietism, 52, 53, 82
pious, 82
poor, 85, 89, 102, 103
power, 4, 14, 26, 37, 42, 60, 70, 81, 82, 87, 96,

99, 104, 106, 113, 114, 122, 126, 135, 140
praise, 41, 61, 85, 128, 130
receptive, 115
rich, 75, 102, 103, 134
rituals, 83
ruler, 64, 74, 79, 84, 115, 117, 132, 134, 139
self-centered, 32, 42, 53
self-control, 42
self-indulgent, 125
self-interest, 17
self-righteous, 110
self-seeking, 42
simplicity, 6, 53, 79
strength to endure, 49, 59, 67, 75, 91, 101
substance, 38, 39, 57, 63, 83, 85, 90, 99
Tao, 4, 5, 9, 13, 14, 15, 20, 21, 22, 23, 24, 27, 28, 31, 33, 37, 44, 45, 46, 47, 49, 52, 56, 57, 58, 59, 60, 61, 62, 63, 64, 70, 71, 72, 73, 74, 76, 77, 79, 82, 83, 84, 85, 86, 87, 88, 89, 93, 94, 95, 99, 102, 103, 104, 107, 113, 114, 117, 118, 122, 124, 126, 128, 131, 132, 136, 140, 141, 144

Tao of heaven, 94
Tao of nature, 60
the wise, 65, 68, 128, 144
Three Treasures, 16, 124, 127
tradition, 7, 8, 9, 83
treasure, 34, 39, 117, 128
trust, 42, 50, 60, 96, 119
uncarved block of wood, 16, 46, 67, 68, 74, 79, 111
unlearn, 95, 121
useful, 38
violence, 72, 73, 89, 106, 127
war, 73, 93, 110, 127
water, 6, 18, 27, 31, 33, 46, 47, 78, 138
wealth, 34, 39, 91, 117, 144
weapons, 72, 110, 127, 142
wisdom, 7, 8, 22, 46, 75, 78, 114, 126
wise up, 23, 25, 26, 29, 30, 32, 39, 59, 66, 69, 94, 96, 110, 112, 119, 120, 121, 123, 128, 129, 130, 137, 138, 144
worry, 25, 54, 55
yield, 46, 59, 78, 86, 90, 102, 138
Yin and Yang, 14, 89

EVERYONE'S TAO TE CHING

Made in the USA
Middletown, DE
16 March 2021